THE BEAUTIFUL IMMUNITY

THE BEAUTIFUL IMMUNITY

KAREN AN-HWEI LEE

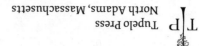
Tupelo Press
North Adams, Massachusetts

Library of Congress Cataloging-in-Publication data available upon request.

ISBN-13: 978-1-961209-07-7 (paperback)   978-1-961209-12-1 (ebook)

Cover and text design by Kenji Liu.

Cover art: Paperweight, c. 1845–60; Cristalleries de Baccarat, Lorraine, France,
founded 1764. Creative Commons Zero, courtesy of The Art Institute of Chicago. Bequest
of Arthur Rubloff.

First paperback edition May 2024

Tupelo Press
P.O. Box 1767
North Adams, Massachusetts 01247
(413) 664-9611 | Fax: (413) 664-9711
editor@tupelopress.org | www.tupelopress.org

Tupelo Press is an award-winning independent literary press that publishes fine fiction,
non-fiction, and poetry in books that are a joy to hold as well as read. Tupelo Press is a
registered 501(c)(3) nonprofit organization, and we rely on public support to carry out
our mission of publishing extraordinary work that may be outside the realm of the large
commercial publishers. Financial donations are welcome and are tax deductible.

This project is supported in part by the National Endowment for the Arts

NATIONAL ENDOWMENT for the ARTS
arts.gov

TABLE OF CONTENTS

3. DEAR MILLENNIUM, ON THE BEAUTIFUL IMMUNITY

4. ON MERIDIANS OF LOVE AND DISTANCE

ACKNOWLEDGMENTS

Grateful acknowledgment is made to the following journals and anthologies where a number of these poems first appeared, some in earlier form.

*

Academy of American Poets (Poem-a-Day): "On Floriography," "Dear Millennium, Inadequate Witness," and "Dear Millennium, on the Angel of Immigration"

The Account: "Dear Millennium, a Jade Rabbit on the Far Side of the Moon" and "Dear Millennium, on the Methuselah Star"

Angel City Review: "Prayer in the Year of No Rain"

Asterix: "On Radio Angels in the Troposphere"

Bone Bouquet: "On the Flavor of Awe" (formerly "Meditation on Awe as Flavor")

Border Voices Anthology edited by Michael Chung Klam, Jack Webb, and Bill Harding: "On Meridians of Love and Distance"

The Collagist: "On the Youngest Filament in the Universe"

Entropy-Enclave: "Postscript to Dear Millennium, Love"

Free Verse: "Prayer at Thirty-Seven Thousand Feet above Sea Level"

Gravity of the Thing: "Dear Millennium, on the Proof of Beauty"

Hampden-Sydney Review: "Meditation on Error as Beauty"

HocTok: "On Levitation at the Carp-Tail Sugar Factory"

Ilanot Review: "Ode to the Longest Pier on the Left Coast"

Image: Art, Faith, Mystery: "On Lectio Divina, Counter-Clockwise," "Meditation on Soteriology," "Irenology," and "Grace in Action or Murphy's Law in Reverse"

Kalyani Magazine: "Meditation on Fruit-Bearing"

Kenyon Review: "Perfume Enfleurage as Awareness," "On Apophasis and the Unnamable," "On Lightening" and "On Radiolucence"

The Massachusetts Review: "Meditation on Skin"

Modern Poetry Quarterly Review: "Dear Millennium, on Nine Orders of Angels"

Moria: "On the Names of Invasive Beauty"

New Madrid: "Zona Negativa" and "Dear Millennium, on the Interior Disclosures"

Ninth Letter: "Nonce Ode to an Oxymoron"

The Normal School: "Prayer for the Lost Water Bees"

North American Review: "A Short Autobiography of Perfume"

Ocelli: "Dear Millennium, Inside a Hummingbird is God"

Oxidant Engine: "Dear Millennium, on Phenomena"

Poetry: "On Hierophany," "On June Blossoming in June," "Ode to the Tiniest Dessert Spoon in All Creation," and "Song of the Oyamel,"

Poetry Northwest: "Dear Millennium, on Weather Alerts as Doxology," "On Reverse Parousia, the Sequel,"

Prairie Schooner: "Seven Cantos on Silence," "Ode to My Namesake on the Other Side of the Universe," "On Lucid Dreaming," "On the Levitation of Beautiful Objects,"* and "On a Lovefeast of Sundays."

A Public Space: "Dear Millennium, on the Debt of Love among Strangers"

Rock & Sling: "Dear Millennium, Our Hungry Roses," "On Apophasis and a Bee," and "Prayer for a Box of Lightning"

Ruminate: "The Silk Lessons" and "On Insect-Holes as Fragrant Portals of Edible Light"

Santa Clara Review: "On Blessing Lentils"

Shanghai Literary Review: "Dear Millennium, on Defamations in the Metropolis"

South Dakota Review: "Dear Millennium, Figs Say Hunger Alone Is Not the Body"

Spoon River Poetry Review: "Fourteen Gratitudes," "On the Turning of the Year," and "Dear Millennium, on Little Valentines as Corpuscles of Love"

Southern Florida Poetry Review: "The Millennial Year of the Superbloom" and "The Last Bookstore in the World"

Uproot: "On Levitation in a Season of Famine" and "Dear Millennium, on Lost Orchards"

Terrain.org: "Dear Millennium, Love" and "Dear Millennium, a Sanctuary"

Virginia Quarterly Review: "Dear Millennium, on Resurrected Beauty" (formerly "On Beauty")

Waxwing: "A Tender Deciphering of Jacaranda"

West Branch: "Meditation on the End of All Things"

Yale Review: "Dear Millennium, of Edible Blossoms and the Unborn"

Yellow as Turmeric, Fragrant as Cloves, edited by Anne-Marie Fowler of Deep Bowl Press: "Petty Skills Like the Carving of Insects" and "Ode to Red Minutes in a Heat Wave"

*"On the Levitation of Beautiful Objects" was subsequently reprinted with the author's permission in *They Rise Like A Wave: An Anthology of Asian American Women Poets.* Edited by Randy White, Christine Kitano, and Alycia Pirmohamed. Rocklin, CA: Blue Oak Press.

MILLENNIAL YEAR OF THE SUPERBLOOM 1

MILLENNIAL YEAR OF THE SUPERBLOOM

In the millennial year of the superbloom, after the ruthless drought—
and shortages: cream-colored and goldenrod and black-eyed daises
flooded over the retro-fitted sea cliffs, bayside and Oceanside
where I spent hours lost on the southern peninsula.

The sun fed blue light into the baleen heart of the surf, reforming
its unstrung, broken freedom in blue guitars of curled azure flame.
Rains revived the sea lettuce and sea fig, bougainvillea, chaparral
understory. I asked a woman how old she would be, twenty years

from this moment, and she whispered with joy, ninety-one
and blooming.

ZONA NEGATIVA

Solo
alight and over—
humming our souls
arisen, a redolence of God,
fragrance, a myrrh residue,
offering splendid zones of salvage—
Is this irresistible grace or blindness?
What language exists after catastrophe?
Is this irresistible grace or blindness?
Offering splendid zones of salvage—
fragrance, a myrrh residue,
arisen, redolence of God
humming our souls
alight and over—
solo.

Solo
over and alight—
souls, our humming
God of redolence arisen,
residue, a myrrh fragrance
salvage of zones, splendid offering.
Is this blindness or irresistible grace?
What catastrophe exists after language?
Is this blindness or irresistible grace?
Salvage of zones, splendid offering
residue, a myrrh fragrance,
God of redolence arisen,
souls, our humming
over and alight—
solo.

MEDITATION ON SKIN

Breathes with you and everything in the room.

Takes a pumice stone to the heels of your feet.

Covers the soul, largest organ of the body.

Mends the world without complaint, a letter.

Lives sweet without strife in one's family.

Arises from gene expression and a pulse.

Shields a book, an envelope, this life.

Seals a wide barrier of continuous resilience

molting and shedding, versatile at night.

Hydrated moon is the sea's motion. Flaring

consciousness foams over a wall,

encloses this phenomenal world at a touch.

Consciousness foams over a wall.

Hydrated moon is the sea's motion, flaring,

molting and shedding, versatile at night.

Seals a wide barrier of continuous resilience.

Shields a book, an envelope, this life.

Arises from gene expression and a pulse.

Lives sweet without strife in one's family.

Mends the world without complaint, a letter.

Covers the soul, largest organ of the body.

Takes a pumice stone to the heels of your feet.

Breathes with you and everything in the room.

ON FLORIOGRAPHY

If you often find yourself at a loss for words
or don't know what to say to those you love,
just extract *poetry* out of *poverty*, this dystopia
             of civilization rendered fragrant,
         blossoming onto star-blue fields of loosestrife,
heady spools of spike lavender, of edible clover
             beckoning to say without bruising
a jot of dog's tooth violet, a nib of larkspur notes,
         or the day's perfumed reports of indigo
           in the gloaming—
     what to say to those
          whom you love in this world?
Use floriography, or as the flower-sellers put it,
Say it with flowers.
—Indigo, larkspur, star-blue, my dear.

DEAR MILLENNIUM, INADEQUATE WITNESS

Say we no longer bear witness to a body-politic of trauma
after revolution
       by anesthesia or erasure. Say we cover our eyes
to crossed olive-wood beams on a hill. Modes of witness
expose our inadequacy, the human. Forgetting
is a sign—yes, a thing once existed. Say we are unworthy
of witness, internal or external—
             our damaged wisdom, for instance,
our diminished capacity for empathy
      and heightened apathy to torture
mingled with doves
       of unfettered desire
         or an eclipsed divine.

DEAR MILLENNIUM, INSIDE A HUMMINGBIRD IS GOD

On a calyx of bougainvillea, a gill of rain on ranunculus,
lamp-colored resin in fire hills of whitebark,

quark as a Falkland name for a black-crowned night heron,
quarks flavoring a quantum universe,

vision of agua vitae in the Mojave, shinbones, grief, or salterios—
only beetle-drilled air rushing the inner ear,

custodian of vertigo. No men coughed ashore, no prophets
swallowed in the flesh, no one else—

ON APOPHASIS AND A BEE

A buttered roll and a dinner bee are not in this line.
Orthography is a roll baked at a spelling contest.
The spotlights on the spellers, I mean, burning
at roll call. See, neither role-play nor dinner rolls.
On apophasis, a translator says, I will only render
what is there, not what is not. For instance,
deus ex machina never appears in the source-text
as a buttered angel-fish or 400-watt flying bicycle
although one might say this poem is an engine.
At no point does a line break exist in the original.
Neither is a hand-held spyglass an engine of words
while *sparrow-grass* spells *asparagus*
　　　　　buzzing in the ear of this language.

ON APOPHASIS AND THE UNNAMABLE

Flame trees or not, apophasis is another way to say no—
No to *Plebejus lupini* washed lilac blue in the hills—
No to a rabble of single-brood butterflies, swimming—
No to hidden lavender bed flourishing on the commons.
No to apophasis as a sly allusion to the unnamable—
How jacaranda, after one night, wet the skin of my hand
without the eschatologies of a post-revelatory hour—
Just as you prayed when we stood in the schoolroom.
No to tousled shag moss under a disheveled mimosa—
To the invisible fishing-twine crossing a wire trellis—
To appellations of mission vineyards, green signatures.
Chaparral does not rhyme with a thousand biomes of ash,
Silver Fire and Esperanza, the Rim Fire, the De Luz Fire—
No to our homes, dreams and visions razed in pure flame.
We invite God to share a word—a prophetic revelation,
a storm of fiery signs for a wayward third millennium
as the Holy Spirit weeps tongues of tangible anointing—
wakening in speech what is already sealed in verse.

MEDITATION ON ERROR AS BEAUTY

The moon's autologous neap-light
            is not even truly its own,
                            bone marrow to bone
                    after the first or third quarter.

Gaslight moon in a veiled floral gyre
                        is not actual lunar shine,
        rather, midnight fire and a salty dash of starlight.

Bowed, I hold one indigo jessamine
            in the hollow of my inner arm, act of mutagenesis
in a hazardous
universe: in half-light, a hawk-moth slows
                its tiny brain to see portals of aroma.

                        Enter. Herein—
micrometers. Of ecstasy.
                Minus one.

ON HIEROPHANY

One example of *hierophany* is the apparition of angels.
This is a new word I overheard this morning. It occurs
when the divine realm manifests—or the word intrudes—
into our quotidian realm. The natural one, an untidy
fleshliness of the ordinary. Or the sacred and profane
is another way to say this. I asked whether it is a hernia,
and the answer was, no. A herniated condition is viscera
on viscera—a disc, organs, the skin or nerves. Besides,
such a comparison would be profane. A figure of speech
already exists, I said, in a hieratic silence of cursive
writing long ago dead. Not long ago, those two phrases
dwelled in separate worlds. I dare you to use the word
hernia in a poem, said a friend. So I not only used
the word, I invited God into language. Or God existed
before language, while God is also the word. Remember,
all theophanies are forms of hierophany. However,
the converse is not always true—not all hierophanies
are theophanies—or God visible in our world.

ON FOURTEEN GRATITUDES

My fortieth year is one of radiolucence—
bluntly, I pressed my rib cage into an x-ray
machine for a mammogram. How I held
my breath while it irradiated this body.

And how it rained *sweet william* in violet.
How black mission figs rotted on a walk,
bruised tattoos—or tea-roses—bleeding.
And I held back-lit vellum to binary stars,

to letterpress clouds drifting on a mall
of flesh humming blue without cologne.
How tissue flowered over forty decades,
four flights of stairs and a final deluge.

How El Niño flooded our foothill arroyos
with *mondegreen* for the slip of a lyric.
How the ocean bleached this sundress
of black pepper, galangal, and sea salt.

How I fed wild doves in outdoor chapels.
Fourteenth gratitude—age forty is not
fourteen reversed, a girl's ambling love
sweeter than the blackest cherry moon,

than a fly-bitten rash of river blindness
singing *light* under a palm-date tree.
Light, the light, a mourning dove
coos in the dusk as well as in light.

A TENDER DECIPHERING OF JACARANDA

If desire foams over a sea-wall, this is non-negotiable—
            let us cease quarrelling about whether jacaranda

ignites lavender perfume under a pilot's skin
            distilled of night blindness and vertigo,

whether you dreamed of a flight rotating counter-clockwise
            on a runway, other side of the bay on fire—

of royal empress trees neither royal nor empress—
            whether what we love will last our whole lives,

those fragrant, ornamental groves of water-loving blossoms,
            or not what we love but rather, how—

whether we carelessly toss *los cigarillos* in gutters,
            save our ash-petaled lungs, or dash to hills

seeking only what we know of tenderness in jacaranda heights,
            —deliverance.

PRAYER FOR THE LOST WATER BEES

The ocean is a crazed blue azalea.
                    Honeybees are intoxicated on blue—
this is why they vanished.

No one knows where the water bees went
          in the heat, since bees are drawn to water.

Others say it is an omen. California will slide into the sea
          where it first belonged, a shelf underwater.

Angelenos call the phenomenon of swarming water bees
          a congregation as in a church- anointed fire.
                    Water bees vanish.

Or say water bees never existed in the first place. This is why
          we do not know where they went. We never knew

their true names or their places of origin. We conjure bees
          drawing water in their bellies, glass bulbs of rain

flying over culverts and arroyos in search of hovels
          to call home. In the light of firehills,

the sun is not rising but setting—dunes illuminated
          by the light of invisible bees—

this is why they vanished.

A SHORT AUTOBIOGRAPHY OF PERFUME

Once upon a grandiflorum,
I was a flash-fire in darkness.
I was glacial phlox.
I was ambergris in a whale's belly,
a bone-spear,
kilos of roses distilled in Asia Minor
                roiling in copper florentines,
a fixative washed ashore—
not an otolith, not ear wax of whales.
I say to ethers and esters—
not yet the skin of a vanilla pod
or red tears of migrant workers.
Not a cuttlefish
       sliced for birds to take home.
Not stolen blood of pines.
Not amber. Not even beeswax

where I survived
as sea-light—
         as spiritual fuel,
pollen oils of *rosa centifolia*,
                your stark rooms of musk
on the waved mile,
your edible field of lavender on this ear,
your covalency of desire
       praised, sung, decanted.

PRAYER AT THIRTY-SEVEN THOUSAND FEET
ABOVE SEA LEVEL

To travel
on a thousand prayers. To say I was blessed as a girl
to fly across the world
                so it no longer holds mystique.

Still, a miracle to ride the air.

To look up weather reports.
To use origami skills, folding clothes to the tiniest size.
To bring a rain parka folded like a wing or not.

To notate the back of a napkin—
ate a quarter of a red-angel pomegranate
                    this afternoon. Tart.

To fly over small orchards, blossom-end.

PERFUME ENFLEURAGE AS AWARENESS

The airport closes due to a broken bottle
of perfume.

       From enfleurage to blossoming paranoia—
illness, waves of nausea. Fixatives and scents,
the aromatic heart

of cinnamon, vanilla, almonds,
bitter orange, oil of bergamot, fruit esters and aldehydes,
           dark seaweed, lilac, and deer musk

in a single whiff. Who knew whale ambergris
       and linalool could create a state of panic

or others might say, a heightened awareness
shielded by fat or wax

                then extracted with ethanol.
Wine, snow globes, and perfume
                  are restricted items
infused with a liquid potential to flame,
even water.

MEDITATION ON FRUIT-BEARING

Reason to open a window at dusk:
    night-blooming jasmine.

Prayer for women:
    hillside eucalyptus. Mist

no higher than my shoulder,
    lemons in a tub:

eye-pupils, one drupe each spring:
    thundercloud plum.

    Hazel tufts in rain
calyx-end or blossom-end:
      mission figs.

Not to cast a woman's fruit:
    blessed, for she is with child.

One word: pomegranates.
    Two words: quince, pear.

Morning sickness, first trimester—
    nine months in sum, we pray

for a woman and her unborn.

Lavender chaos on the road:
    jay-walking for jacaranda.

Yet to see a flowering almond.

Yet to see in groves—
    light falling in stanzas.

PRAYER FOR A BOX OF LIGHTNING

Forget how the agave gives two-story spike blossoms
once in a lifetime before dying. Pray for the bees
who abandoned their abode by a utility box of lightning,
evidence of their glass-radiant itinerancy by association,
the high voltage of residual gold in a hive of eyes open,
eyes closed, cells in monochrome—no one to bleed
electricity as honey. The giant agave, the utility box
is one and the same shade—sea-foam, emerald, cerulean,
azul for heaven—or say, celadon. Jade-veined. Sage
in tone or value, succulence more tender than our mesa
rolling out a new summer line of bolero dresses
lingering in the flushed ash-rosettes of Jurupa Valley—
a hundred twelve degrees on asphalt. Sun-fevered,
we walk outside our skin, rain-sweet agave
by lightning.

ON THE NAMES OF INVASIVE BEAUTY

Jagged tussock of seed, razored fire-fountain,
the hair-length awn of burnished gold, needle
finished with a silk-smooth pod called a lemma
tethered in the sand, germinating on air-bright
silica, a corona or miniature seed-crown latches
to my sleeve as I thin the rampant vine-runners
under the avocado. Burred, sun-kissed spikelet,
part hook, part sail, ornamental Nassella species,
a renowned invasive beauty, part foil-kite, part
switchblade, angled spawn of drought-resistant
angels settled on bougainvillea glow-torches,
in the fissures of decomposed snow-granite,
dormant seed-bank with a mission to invest
without usury, without a return of premium—
dear imported kin, do forgive the xenophobia
against our heat-loving, wire-grass beauties—
rather, let us all endure as naturalized migrants
in this incendiary history of exclusion. A wind
lifts tufted feathergrass to a sloped flagstone
terrace edged by salt river rock, where we settle
with minimal demand on an indigenous scape.

PRAYER IN THE YEAR OF NO RAIN

The year I turned forty coincided with the worst drought
in California since I moved west, if not for decades.
Over a thousand trees in the oldest arboretum west
of the Mississippi flailed in thirst. Fish died of salinity—
saltwater intrusion in rivers. Aerial photos of the Sierras,
unceremonious earth-skinned aridity. Only a cycle,
while others said, global warming. El Niño will return.
Eco-prophets shall construct their arks of gopherwood
in the high desert, miles away from closed fishing piers
and hatcheries where young salmon, wayfarers pooling
on a layover flight, will delay spawning. I said a prayer
for rain at the swimming pool, wrung water out of my hair
with bare hands as if each misty strand might quell fever
by refusing to drink.

GRACE IN ACTION OR MURPHY'S LAW IN REVERSE

Anything that can go wrong,
will go wrong. It is what the law says.
However, the summer of our prayers
was one of grace in action. An outage
from nine in the morning until three
in the afternoon never quite elapsed
despite all the signs. I witnessed utility
men working in the street as well as
silenced air conditioning in a bodega.
This was summer, yet late autumn
Santa Anas were already blowing miles
east out of the high desert, sparking
chaparral in the foothills and arroyos.
Later, I bought a ten-pound bag of ice
because five pounds wasn't enough.
I couldn't carry twenty pounds home.
An unnamed woman held out her hand
like a traffic guard asking me to stop
at the crosswalk. I stopped. A vehicle
flashed by the parked armored van.
She saved my life, this angel who said—
Ten pounds of ice float on a heat wave
in a city where all the refrigerators died
in a rolling blackout that never occurred
because Murphy's law—in reverse—
operated as grace in action. Your ice
box, on the other hand: God incarnate,
fire and ice burning simultaneously.
If anything can go wrong, it will,
so open the door—stand in the light.

ODE TO MY NAMESAKE ON THE OTHER SIDE OF THE UNIVERSE 2

ODE TO MY NAMESAKE ON THE OTHER SIDE
OF THE UNIVERSE

A woman with the same name as mine
lives on the other side of the universe—
probing non-small cell lung disease,

microscopic radial scars, magnetic
resonance imaging, liquid diagnostic
platforms for biopsies, designing

new cures in her field of cancer
medicine. As Karen's counterpart,
a poet on this side of the universe,

I wonder if angels hover in her room
at night, humming while messengers
soar under low evening clouds, laughing

in a swirl of lucid dreaming, updrafts
soaked in the intoxicating perfume
of mad honey flowing out of portals

of lost Karens—extinction of doves,
the vestiges of sea-faring pilgrims,
polar ice caps melting by degrees,

the delirium of time itself flung
in starry vectors of the inevitable
shot through to the survival

of eponymous women like us, how
we could've lived if we were not
marooned on this side of fate.

THE LAST BOOKSTORE IN THE WORLD

In the last bookstore in the world—
on the last shelf

in the last aisle,
a volume of poetry—

invisible. No long-nosed flies,
no moth fur,

no silverfish
No underlined word—

sentience

where I put a feather
found on Sunday

by accident or inheritance,
coincidence

or divine appointment.
Only a dollar per used copy,

hold a quill to light.

ON THE LEVITATION OF BEAUTIFUL OBJECTS

For those who desire one, here is a tale. Once upon a tropical storm, in my turbulent years as a weather system, I was a typhoon named Karen. If I whirled my spiral rainbands in the north, my rotation would've shifted to the right. In reality, the Coriolis Effect deflected my movement in the southern hemisphere.

A corrective footnote in meteorological history, for the record—

I made landfall as a tropical storm, not a hurricane
      by the Isla de la Juventad, the Isle of Youth.
         On this archipelago, I alighted on an isle,
   kissed the gangly mangrove shores,
     upset ferries, hydrofoils, yachts.

While serenity blew a puff of air—a test in my solo eye—I roared no to sea ports and unreeled an archive of 35 mm film, no to fashion institutes, no to civil engineering, no to female pelvic exams, no to forced sterilization, no to acid vibes of the bay, absolutely no to war, a decolonial no to imperialism. A thousand megawatts powering a million off-shore turbines,

I tossed a love note into my namesake storm—

Dear brazen fury of *juventad*, I lost strength while summoning the beauty of the unanchored, not the lost. Pure verticality and relentless power, as the world's rudest tambourine, I dragged my inclemency over palmetto groves, fishing piers, and utility lines. Beloved denizens of the archipelago, so very anthropocentric in scope, you failed to see

I was only levitating beautiful objects.

ON LEVITATION AT THE CARP-TAIL SUGAR FACTORY

As if the levitation of miniature objects is a surprise—
                         scale isn't a miracle of perception
                                     or fruit of anti-gravity:
a robin's egg on the palm of my hand, aloft in June—
                 bird-soul's turquoise bell. Tetrapyrrolic molecules
yield a color, biliverdin, to new bruises:
                      a blue-rayed moon
                mined out of mineral vapor, stabilized
     with resin for excavated turquoise.
Ferrous cataracts shine in a slit-lamp, ranging from viridian
                        to cloudy milk-blue, star of India.
Chin of a scallion floats in the shallows
within earshot of the old Hualien sugar factory where girls sell bottles
       of lemongrass oil.
                      Our typhoon sky levitates miniature things—
          starlings, fish, prawns, algae—a rainstorm bluing
porphyry, of epochal longevity in rhyolite.
       Only the sequential names
of the mill exist: Carp-Tail Sugar Factory, Taiwan Harbor Sugar Company,
                no more war bombings and sugar production.
Out of a greening core of biliverdin, of bile drops in ducts,
exogenous blood—fragile bone-case of bruises,
                        waterfall ink swirling in flesh—
           vigor of a spirit-fountain of blue dye.
       All this to say, I touched a robin's egg this June—
               verily, so light, it floated on a prayer:
                     do you believe?

ANAGRAMS OF SILENCE IN THE REALM OF ANGELS

What forces bind us together, our atoms of silence
           in anagrams? A *fleecer lightness, lemons, melons*—
apples of gravity, a zillion quarks fluttering
           in orchard moonlight. *An elegiacal freshness, molten,*
allegiances enmesh florets, a misfeasance, gentler hellos—
Of course, it's a realm of silent angels rearranged,
                a miracle lenses glen, a lace mill greenness—
motionless roses furled in hematite,
           for all I know. Mystery, an iron-rose ore
blossoming out of a rhombus. Can't see it like the soles
               of my bare feet as I walk in the superbloom
of a spring arroyo. As a girl, I worried if I couldn't sleep
           before the sun rose, I would die, as if death
wouldn't fish a soul out of a sleeping body, as well—
           not waken. Ninety million miles from the sun,
whether we wish to believe or not, our planet weeps
           a new rosary of unsaid prayers
                in a realm of angels,
a cleanse linger elms, a liner nacelle gems—seraphim
in syllogisms of air. Syllable on syllable, metamorphoses
           mold an orthoclase of feldspar—
glorious, joyful, sorrowful, the luminous mysteries
              of tectosilicate masses, an earthquake
         weathering under a nonverbal perfume,
            floral ethers and fruity esters,
anagrams unveiled. *A graceless linen elm,*
           a glance serene mills, a recall lessening me—
upcycled silver butterflies, the filigree buffed
            with foil, hot water, and a paste of baking soda
                in reverse oxidation. A black pearl of silence,
six-millimeter heart, its nacre opaque as spherules
of blueberries on Mars—How did they get there, and why?
                 What makes strangers fall in love
or drift apart like planets in tectonic shifts of distance,
           intimacy, temperament, or kindness—
              molecular fragrance. Pheromones.

Transparency. Self-revelation. Rearrangement of an alphabet
for this rough existence—
    or the lighting of heat lamps for greenery.

NONCE ODE TO AN OXYMORON

How could I ever love such a contrary figure of speech?
Say we never vowed ourselves to a neurosis of nonce verse,
       of fever chills or brazier darkness.
Say we drove to a landlocked shore, rolled up our windows at night,
listened to the bright surf pounding cold and black in the wind.
Say at a tropical storm's landfall we lashed ourselves to blindness
or ate skinned tilapia fillets in a cantina
sans canteens, only brightening shades in a triangular square
       once a man or woman's living quarters—
say this man and woman once were us, eating out of bowls
of seafood paella, of fresh jade mussels from a mobile stand.
And you wondered aloud,
       why not *food of the sea* to avoid potential ambiguity
       about nourishing the ocean or vice versa?
Dear oxymoron, my beloved, you embody nothing apart
       from contradictions or incongruities
as the words tourniquet and sobriquet do not rhyme.
       Say beet after beet rolled on our unsown garden
after we labored, post-storm. Say we ate the darkest moonlit ganache
on the grass and never argued—say, whether it was
a flourless chocolate torte or flat cacao round. Say we tossed dishes
of dogged catfish dispassionately with feline zeal.
Let us say it—*love* pervaded everything we said or did—reedy stanzas
       of unfixed antistrophes—of hand-torn melodrama
the brackish color of misery. Say we loved each another even
       if we could only say its opposite.

SEVEN CANTOS ON SILENCE AS VIA NEGATIVA

CANTO 1.

(Neither is the word silence equivalent to the loveliest of lovely days
       beginning with love and lengthening with the light
           where an open parenthesis never closes—

CANTO 2.

Neither is it an invisible flock of small n-dashes
          flying in hyphens of horizontal light to a skyline
where little nothings brush the air with em-dashes
          as pauses or broken spaces
              and caesuras where sound vanishes
in a pear-shaped curve of the world, this eardrum
     pushing against the reverberation of cold winter light on the floor—
          pupils dilating in the unfastened ink of the dark.

CANTO 3.

The fog in a green church of wind on the sea cliff—

CANTO 4.

In a grove, feral lorikeets in a red-gum eucalyptus
fall silent, awed
       by a solar eclipse in winter—sunlight
             dims in a kelp forest
where swimmers drowned, their legs tangled by ribbons
of silence,
       undersea deaths by apnea—

CANTO 5.

Phenomena in antithesis to silence—
         white noise of engines spinning in turbines,
     a dial tone on a rotary telephone the color of oranges,
thunder rolling over foothills, signposts telling the miles ahead,
     and a memory of sweet-tongued heat

pooling in a jar of early summer marmalade,
pink lemons whose rose-quartz flesh shouted with honey—
                    maddening honey of sugar and roses, a mineral
matrix of molten sweetness.

CANTO 6.

          Silence is a dashed grammar of punctuated roses,
brackets blossoming without desire
          for closure, or fragrant elision and contraction,
                    ellipses in the motion of an eye
          petaling across quartos folded
                         one inside the other as mutual offerings.
For a spring season, I wait on God to speak a word,
                    i.e. blooming, blooming, blooming—
                    wherein I also learn how God replies
in the manner of an open parenthesis
                              which is no sound at all. *(My presence
will go with you, and I will give you rest—*

CANTO 7.

The quietest room in the world is not silence.
          The word silence is not silence.
Such irony—cantos on silence
                    verb and verb so much sound.

ON A LOVEFEAST OF YESTERDAYS

No word for the scent, we say, on a road of dips
on our way to the sweetest spot in the foothills
where we ate spice cookies aerial, thin as autumn
gingersnaps baked right next to the blacksmiths,
a hedge-maze by a church with an acre cemetery—
none of it tasted bitter, rather, sweet without smoke
swirling in our lungs, without honey-laced beeswax,
nor the rolled cigars lying asleep in their boxes
for shipment, nor barrels of molasses, nor hickory,
not tar or nougat or malt whiskey, not gingersnaps
or chocolate chess pie or black sugar. We relish
a lovefeast of yesterdays, pin up elusive syllables
of fragrance wafting through avenues in search
of loaves or leaves cured in bakeshops, the houses
of shivering air elusive as an aroma of nostalgia—
mulching a ferny floor in the hills, a festive crush
of tobacco drying with a brisk sweetness of angels
observing us with eyes on a world where the name
of a thing is not the thing itself.

ON LEVITATION IN A SEASON OF FAMINE

Are we in a raging famine, dear millennium?

              The four-year drought ruins our agronomy—*cara cara* oranges, fig orchards of inverted blossoms, jailed heads of butter lettuce, cotton bales, parable-worthy vineyards of signature chardonnay. In a faux equation of reverse alchemy,

        the fool's gold of meadow barley, *Hordeum brachyantherum*, mints vaults of bullion.

        A woman of financial projections and eschatological prophecies advises us to store food supplies for six months. *Six months*, I echo. *Half a year?*

Famine is the last pumpkin in the field, a curling vine
        cleaved open like a Heian daybook,
                      boiled with congee porridge,
           pepitas roasted with iodized salt,
the sun's gold tooth gnawing on a rind of hunger.

Where I would store half a year's worth of provisions, never mind what I would buy, if I could? Circulars in the month of June say what I see: migrating *Nymphalidae* in overhead waves,

        virga rain soothing a cursory dusk,
          cumulonimbus in untouched aqueous rows
              playing a forty-note glass harmonica,
          a verrophone sky
              of upcycled flutes and pipes.

ON LAUGHTER IN A GARDEN, POST-CATASTROPHE

A fiddlehead unfurls a fleecy, coiled question
                    in our future. Did we ever foretell
calamity in a garden of succulents—cholla, prickly pear,
            echeveria up to our shoulders, a topiary hedgehog
                    of shapely cactus irradiated by starlight?
Who presaged the unfolding of catastrophe?
Did we ever come here, before we knew one other?
                    Our botanical monograph of stills in memory—
        jacaranda in bloom, a gorgeous mess
on the pavement, and a long-haired violinist
                    who stepped shyly out of greenery
    for the sole purpose of recording
                    an audio of timeless lyric
with murmurs of water splashing from pool to pool
            in late echoes of afternoon light
where we wondered if we could use the word *lyric*
                    without invoking an anachronism—
    in the garden, at the height of a lamb's chin,
                a gnomon darkens a telltale sliver of time
    with a shadow, nearly motionless, while the sundial
hums a speechless whimsy in a world of noise
                    contrary to voices and the visible,
                    so vulnerable to verdigris—
    we spoke to a copper sundial to call on womankind,
                    our sisters in the desert, our mothers on the coast
evoking laughter not yet forgotten in a season of grief—
            yes, this afternoon, we return to an elemental good,
    of rosemary crisps kissed by fig butter, an orchid tree
of elegiac lamps offered by those who love us,
            how light is loaned to us from God—
wherein light, mingled with the unsaid,
        is a form of silent laughter, of mirth and mystery alike.
This is poetry, how we reenter the human—
            how we partake of this bread of mutual presences
made out of a door of flesh, of souls in mud unhinged
        by the hands of a holy presence, the maker of all things

who gathers the crushed hulls of jacaranda
on this fragrant lane riddled
with scraps of beauty and strife.

SONG OF THE GREEN FLASH

As we sped eastward over the freeway at sunset
to red-violet and indigo bands of a rainband
       loudest, sweetest, closest to our awe,

a lemongrass sprig in a chilled bottle of water—
you said, *Never seen the sky like this all the times*
       I've passed this way—

I said, *It's a glory cloud, the Holy Spirit sailing*
      above our heads, joy unfolding
         in a liquid orb of love
      overflowing westward
as we dashed from the cove to Mount Soledad, sea cliffs—
updrafts of evening wind on a soft ledge—
I pointed my elbows skyward like a pelican—
        you said, *if only we could bottle this sunset.*
I said, *have you ever seen the green flash?*
It appears a second before the sun dips
below the skyline, a handsome emerald flashing
       on the finger of a film actress.
Those who see the green flash, the legend says,
are immune to folly in matters of the heart—
wise in the ways of love.

     Now I muse, it's hard to put dusk in a jar,
yet this stanza is room enough for all the good in our lives—
God's *poemas* of souls, this glorious handiwork,
     a palette of cirrus and rose-gold waves,
      prisms of lotus afloat on ponds, lilies of the valley,
tide pools ringing the sky like watered silk
adorned with butterfly knots, your mother's prize camellias,
     aureoles in rays of light rain
while tender boats of night turned their prows back to shore—
the waves rushing onto the sands, withdrawing
and you, hushed as wisteria under your breath
     in a holy wood dropping fragrance around us,
waited to see if I would match

the resonance of another pulsing heart—
if this would be the moment, or this one,
or this one.

ON RADIOLUCENCE

How can you tell if the God of the universe
shines in a thing as odd as a soul?
              I mean the weary souls we pass on the street
on the way to work in the morning. The soul in line
at the bank or a cashier in the grocery store.
The soul riding a bicycle lashed together by string,
              a fishing pole over one shoulder.
Do fish have souls?
Can we see it peering out from a carp's gold iris
or a hooked eye weeping silver?
              The apostle says we are treasures
in jars of clay. Our souls, I guess, in *casas* of flesh.
We are diamonds in the rough until we pass trials
of fire and water. Our souls come without inborn
tickets to heaven, and admission cannot be earned,
only freely given.
              Breathe on a diamond to see
if it is authentic. See whether a diamond cuts glass
and fluoresces under ultraviolet light. Did you
know that scorpions also fluoresce this way?
What does it mean if diamonds and scorpions
glow alike in blacklight—
                            a hyaline layer of skin
over a soul? What can we shed or confess
so God may live in our souls? What is counterfeit
and what is genuine? Do not use an x-ray machine.
Diamonds and souls are radiolucent, transparent
on the radiograph. Shine a light to see
whether haloes form.

ODE TO THE TINIEST DESSERT SPOON
IN ALL CREATION

In a new translator's version of Genesis, there's no Adam.
No serpent. In paradise, I don't bleed. Fig leaf-free girl,
dear God, I say as we converse fluently without tongues,
joined as two spice-drenched beloveds in a song of songs,
could we ask the gardener to plant a pomegranate grove
by a stand of non-fruiting olive cultivars, which don't bloom
and aren't so messy? Honey, I am the gardener, says God,
whose anthropomorphic footfalls caress the afternoon cool.
Wolves in our botanical garden ask nothing of any human,
eyes the hue of clementines plucked green off a young tree,
one of five in my orchard, per telltale ringless left finger—
fig, clementine, kumquat, oroblanco, and lemon. If I reside
in paradise, then I get to eat all the fruit I want, all day long.
No problem, says God, who calls me a little pouch of myrrh.
An eagle locks eyes with mine. A dove by the pool adores
the wolves as she coos, *gold-amber,* one stone's throw away.
Each one carries a scent: snowy owls of shuttered skies, elk,
bobcats, melanin-rich skin of a feckless human. In paradise,
wolves and doves co-exist. Once, a clementine sat forgotten
in my purse until it acquired the spots of a leopard. A world
in a lion's eye is kohl-lined gold. Aloes and sage carve a path
through a brushy stand of Joshua trees, one which God made
after lightning struck the agave and scrub oak. Joshua trees
are chuppah arches double-wreathed with burrs, scales, fur.
Joshuas aren't guys, so yucca moths activate their ovaries.
Wolves do not question why a male is missing in paradise.
Yes, yucca moths take care of it. Coyotes do not question
the human. Why I'm not married, why childless, howling,
and whether we've reached the century when God invents
a gossamer mousse garnished with absinthe-laced cherries
served in hand-fired ceramic espresso cups, a dessert to taste
together for the first time after we invent a miniature spoon
no larger than a bee-hummingbird, tiniest in all creation.

ON RADIO ANGELS IN THE TROPOSPHERE

Engineers of faltering air, not the radio angels

tighten struts, bolts, and cantilevers of eternal design. Angels
guard antique equipment, invented in principle by our original
architect, eternal logophile, and alpha-omega *abba*.

Shoulders of unseeded rain encircle the troposphere, sweet jaggery
of ferns. Northern lights, the auroras, riff magnetic jazz above the
poles. A low-frequency hum

        signals human civilization or vice versa—

The long winter salts a tangible road of devotion. *Please tune in.*
Do you hear me? Radio angels neither hunger nor thirst: *Tune in.*
Desiderata of coronal flares, gore-rubies of salvation.

No one sees who is there
– lights on
        hovering afield.

ON THE FLAVOR OF AWE

1.

Roused, a female goes into labor, no seed but her own
    and God's.
       This must be a miracle.
The woman's bones creak open—eye of a ferris wheel.
Sheep stop ruminating to listen. In our imminent new world,
   Dinner will not be served in a while, she thinks
as the afterbirth follows.
      An angel applies an herbal balm, angelica root
   and burdock against puerperal fever.

2.

In a technophile future, Jesus dwells in a city of stainless
globally positioned ice-cream machines, *vox populi.*
   Be not mistaken: The Holy Spirit is not a machine
     yet the cogs and levers hum with glory.
Oil the color of cold-pressed olives. Oil the color
       of praline syrup in vanilla.
The ice-cream machines light up a fortress of those
    who taste and see that God is good.

3.

Centuries later, a sinkhole yawns open
   under a railroad.
Quarrels over turf and the nature of signs—
    God wants us to stop breaking things
     and vandalizing creation.
In this millennium, we are no more adept at sacrifice
than we are about saving ourselves
or prophesying *strawberry*
    will appear twice in a poem.

4.

This all to say
at the parlor of vintage lamps and stained glass,

there is a flavor named awe.

        For a dollar more, add foaming
root-beer or sarsaparilla. A woman with a halo—
or an angel— scoops strawberry cookie gelato,
light streaming

        through one-way glass.
What is the flavor of unmerited grace?
Just whisper *hosanna* into a pound of divinity
when no one is listening.

IRENOLOGY

Irene, a girl's name, an emerald. Irenology, peace studies.
How does peace circulate
                              as a form of curriculum?

Open in Ezra and paging to Nehemiah,
          I contemplate exiles rebuilding temple walls.

I thought, is this a form of peace studies?

Confess our sins. Our inability to perform
          a divine-ordained task in our own strength.

Rejoice in God's favor and presence. Carry fragrant
beams of cedar.

Cherish silver and gold restored to our possession.

                    As we lay hands on our settlements,
walk through ruined spaces where our ancestors once lived.

In open air, stand in circles and weep.

          The circles grow larger until they break open
to join one circumference.

Motion of light. God unseals bottles of effervescence
                    silent all these years, now singing.

Yes, the light is still there. Holy Spirit.

Effervescence pours a gold river over our fields. Overflows.

The alpha and omega, *as deep calls to deep,* still there.
In the wilderness.

Let us now call this our home.
                              From peace to praise.
Selah.

THE SILK LESSONS

1. THE FIRST SILK LESSON

Silk lesson number one. First, peace silk
is wild silk. Peace silk does not sacrifice
the fond lives of juvenile mulberry moths.
The cycle of instar to imago is seamless—
the moth emerges. Harvest only broken
cocoons unspun for their silk. Filaments
shorter than sericulture adhered to beauty,
neither peace nor wilderness—nor artifice,
strand after strand, invisible without judging
unraveled lines prior to human ransacking
or rebirth—the latter, a sheer cruelty-free
equivalence.

2. THE SECOND SILK LESSON

The second silk lesson. Not everything said
about silk is true. The empress, for instance,
who loved to hear the sound of tearing silk.
True or false? There is a *qigong* move called
silk. The opposite move is iron. True or false.
Silkworms no longer exist in the wild due to
overharvesting. Use over a thousand cocoons
to reel one pound of silk. If no wild silk exists,
then use peace silk where the pupa matures
to the imago stage and breaks out of the cocoon
rather than dying in hot water. This is still,
however, a form of cultivated silk
or human sericulture.

3. THE THIRD SILK LESSON

The third silk lesson. Old silk, when weathered,
assumes the coppery rue of pennies. Calendered
or watered silk has nothing to do with water.
This is like saying *the light is* without saying
the word light or comparing it to another noun

ending arbitrarily in three consonants. Not
transparent things like a glasswing *mariposa*,
espejitos or little mirrors, the salpas of the sea,
texture of your sister's hair over her shoulder
as she washes. Not the sound of your harp at rest
in a walk-in closet while you sleep with summer
windows open, an electric fan stirring.

4. THE FOURTH SILK LESSON

The fourth silk lesson. *Liang* sheen
of waves mean nothing unto itself.
Nonetheless, if silk could see its image
in a mirror and respond to its name,
then silk would say, *reel me into skeins,
then press me into books. Remember
nothing of my original flesh in nature,
the mulberry moth. Rather, recall me
as a simulacrum of your other self,
the one who never wished to leave
paradise. I clothe a loss of innocence
with my own manufactured skin.*
In this case, if silk is synthetic fiber,
it is neither genetically modified
nor immortal, nor immune to death,
nor this mutable skin of inheritance.

5. THE LAST SILK LESSON

The last silk lesson. When real silk burns,
it does not emit a pleasant fragrance.
Rather, it emits an odor like burning hair.
When you touch a flame to real silk,
it only burns when the flame touches it.
Real silk does not burn apart from fire.
On the contrary, faux silk will go on burning.
Real silk will turn to ash while faux silk
will melt like a lampshade, ardor
of blazing polymer factories.

PETTY SKILLS LIKE THE CARVING OF INSECTS

for the Chinese immigrants detained on Angel Island

1. *Intimate wealth acquired at a great price.*

I sense the ocean change into a mulberry grove.

The violet sea of trees, without reason, and rustling of silk

wake me in the evening; a stranger's words,

like a hundred silkworms, excrete a grove of riches;

this is an ocean, the intimate wealth of a forest.

2. *Prison of a recollected sea.*

I am groves of water and bone, hushed sea of leaves

wavering as the writing brush divides water,

enfolding words to twilight—ink grove

where insects perish, parting without emotion,

lucid desert, prison of a recollected sea.

I have no words to murmur against the east wind.

3. *The ocean is a cell.*

Observe the imprisoned bloom,

an uninterrupted work of writing

linking the center and periphery.

The ocean is a cell to all;

the salt on the sill, dear to you,

creating half the difference,

since you are the salt on the sill.

4. *Detainment.*

Rotating like the arms of a mulberry

in a room where no one lives, no spirit breaks,

one woman's sick chamber is left; no one carves

or heaves over a stool. I imagine frankly

what the angels used for carving—

swords, one stroke at a time,

diagramming the heart of this prison—only

my body is detained in this building.

5. *Two letters for one.*

Now all the angels have quietly left

except the words. As a writing brush tosses free,

I remember how dipping the brush in water

secretes transparency. Angels are invisible,

two letters replaced by one. Invincible

because the wood there was softer.

6. *Radical root of the word.*

It was not easy finding space on the wall.

Carve the radical root of the word,

root of the island where one fissure existed—

break in a cave to let in the morning

looking upon labyrinthine streets;

a fissure of light aroused open visions,

wherever the hand could reach.

7. Even if it is built of jade, it has turned into a cage.

Look at the wounds in my hands and my feet.

I was a witness, a prophet, one crying out in the desert—

no labyrinthine streets existed; I carved them

into being, for the sea has no clear roads

to the inexperienced eye. Even the eye of the insect

is trained to see certain routes, as the hand of the sailor

masters the knots for mooring a ship

in which the slightest movements are supervised.

ON INSECT-HOLES AS FRAGRANT PORTALS OF EDIBLE LIGHT

On the culinary materiality of sacred texts: asterisks of star-anise. Post-devotionals with bytes for millennial career women. The hypothetical verbs of Jesus dyed in beet-juice. Versions centuries apart in age yet millimeters apart in columns, milligrams of sepia ink. Self-pronouncing versions with phonetic spelling. Fig-cakes, gluten-free. A verbatim translation aiming for formal not dynamic equivalence: i.e. bread of life not breadfruit.

Illumination by scribes who transcribed after washing iceberg lettuce or mending rucksacks. Gall-wasp, not sepia ink, for vegetarians. Edible versions dropped as leaflets from hydroplanes or read on the sly with the aid of night-vision binoculars. Hunger, the holy scriptures tongued as honey. Pearloid. Oyster-free translations adorned with inlaid synthetic mother-of-pearl.

Rapacious dung beetles feast on pages of heaven, the literal bread of life. Lignin-rich pulp of trees, food-of-insects devoured as ounces of ambrosia. Anaphoras, plural chiasmi, and acrostics perfumed by the ink of berries. Palatable boustrophedonic version running left to right, right to left. Scrolls in clay jars found by a nomad-shepherd, papyri riddled with insect-holes of edible light.

ODE TO RED MINUTES IN A HEAT WAVE

Birds fly in with cool monsoon winds one month late for the planting of rice fields. A child carries a red umbrella to school and spends the day sleeping underneath the budded octopus tree. A woman sews red flowers on a string, a half-grown girl carries a stack of dry grass in a heat wave. Unrelated to the solar flare, poised electromagnetic: a nuclear red persimmon, protean fusion and whipping field lines, faculae cooling in pale spots, corona hotter than the world, presents one molten red psalm on a rotating arm of the galaxy.

DEAR MILLENNIUM, ON THE BEAUTIFUL IMMUNITY 3

DEAR MILLENNIUM, ON THE BEAUTIFUL IMMUNITY

Dear millennium, you never promised to give me
a full strawberry moon, or amnesty from bioexile,

or genetically modified honey and roasted
stone fruit. Will the moon fall out of the sky?

I never asked you for a pail of peaches rich
in immune-boosting minerals, or a remedy

for autoimmune psoriasis. Wedding bells
never rang for us because you say all's fair

in love and war, your greenhouse methane
outgassing our carbon monoxide emissions

with gusto. Please don't feel obliged to love me
back. Instead, grant me a beautiful immunity

to viral strains with evolved vaccine resistance—
zika of fetal microencephaly, chronic fatigue

syndrome, plagues of dyspepsia and dysthymia
in the nervous weather of vulnerability—

please give me a break from coronavirus,
from your stark xenophobia. Millennium,

don't worry about loving me until death do us part—
I'm immune to your pathologies, my dear.

DEAR MILLENNIUM, ON RESURRECTED BEAUTY

I say to the lily asphodel,
                    onionweed—

How do you bear so much love
in this raw glow?

                    Blackberries
and bees swarm against our home.

Night carries an odor of the Mojave
flowing down from the high desert.

Full moon ails with a gouged eye,
and the sea, with its cool upwelling,

tosses and turns to the west.
        What must I do to earn a living

on this earth? I confess the one
who perished and was buried

rose again. Angels and stones
quaked

            to yield new April light.

DEAR MILLENNIUM, ON PHENOMENA

On phenomena, not phenomenal, as in the virtue
of *dynamis* or dysmenorrhea healed. Phenomena
of nickel-iron meteorites caress a bushfire skyline
in fragments no larger than olives, flesh-stones
knifed in a father's boyhood. Sun-black olives,
dense bodies of phenomenology, fall to the earth
and wild birds come eat. Our bleeding human
phenotypes are only kinsfolk not stone. Girlhood
resurrects a non-fruiting cultivar while saplings
enseed mortal reiterations of winter. Of tree soil
virginal in the pit of an olive. *Oliveras. Olivas.*

DEAR MILLENNIUM, ON LOST ORCHARDS

Once we ate oranges navel-first, blossom-end
in flickering orchard light, a spring rainstorm—
sinkhole of fallenness where an underground
cenote raged, dissolving our quicklime bones,
the first paradise. Post-utopia topiary without—
do not fret about class, neither the one percent
nor the ninety-nine. Now we all live in poverty.
In our former lives, the word *post* did not exist.
Nightly, we used to fish pearls out of aquariums
miraculously filled by God's wheeling ophanim,
on the fire-wings of seraphs, *the burning ones.*
Post-utopia, we gather a thousand fragments
out of a vexed universe in this life, at this time—
post-utopia, love exists in a vacuum, if it exists
in the dirt of nervous chaos tainted by toxic
arsenic, cesium, and loss—
where we cannot say starlings or oranges
once winged the air
        after dark—now and forever,
        dear orchard

DEAR MILLENNIUM, ON SIGNATURES

No vineyards flourish on this sea cliff
overlooking a beach. I dove off the coast
from a ridge of blackberries, midnight

of darkest blackberry wine, sparkling
carbonated stars ringing with music
of the spheres in astronomical arias,

vintage hymns no longer burning.
The fog horns were blowing at sea
away from our wineries up north,

green signatures safe from brushfires.
In a dream of this millennium, I pick
moondrop and sapphire, then syrah

and roussane, colorful names for girls,
petit chablis and meursault les tillets,
pinot noir of chalk grafted with gouais,

champagne de fleury, domaine bousquet.
With the frost, I bottle-age the fruit
frozen in clusters on crystal stems,

ice wine wherein the water solidifies
yet the blood of the fruit, its sweetness
runs through, silky and mellifluous.

DEAR MILLENNIUM, ON LITTLE VALENTINES AS CORPUSCLES OF LOVE

Dear millennium, whisper in my ear, *sarsaparilla,*
        or else say *silliest vanilla* ten times fast. Say
our love is darker, spicier than rosin or chocolate—
        or an imaginary pathos of objects, their clandestine goals
        haunting a garage of lost miscellanea at night—
Our hybrid music of spheres, in this millennium,
        is a data-driven cacophony
of little valentines networking,
of unhewn violins
        glowing neon in their heartwood vaults.
And if a rose-colored oboe exists only in name,
        carved out of roses in any tongue, does it bloom
out of phloem, xylem, rings of dendrochronology,
and ascend, tasting
        liters of sweet nothingness?
Shall we tarry, dear millennium, over a fleck of star dust
           riding a horsehair of light
        as micro-corpuscles of love
        bind our cosmos in theory,
        a four-chambered orchestra
            in a fleet of affections from God?

DEAR MILLENNIUM, ON THE PROOF OF BEAUTY

Exiled, does beauty pose hypotheses without solutions,
      i.e. only a desire to prove thingness-as-beauty
or vice versa? If I say a bowl of radish kimchi is gorgeous,
this is not a proof. Or if I say, bless this head of *baechu* cabbage,
      seasoned with scarlet flakes of *gochugaru*, it is a performative
utterance. (Bury it in the winter ground.) Dear millennium, a verb
           alone proves nothing underground.
If I say, exhume the frozen, uncracked kimchi urn
big enough to ferment the bridled chaos of girlhood—
              blood-honey of subterranean
ripening as an object of transformation, then what ensues,
        dear millennium?
        Let's open this jar of red spices, of anaerobic organisms,
           of your flaming antidote to famine
                to call it grace.

DEAR MILLENNIUM, A SANCTUARY

If we no longer know what it means to be human,
everything here is carnal, souls vetted to survive
fire-bombings, night raids, annihilations of love.
Whom shall we trust, what camaraderie exists?
Truth or dare. No one creates beauty here; desire
nothing. War is no beautiful thing. Not a curative.
Truth: girl once said to me, your body is designed
to heal alone. Algal sea fog rolling every noon is no
remedy for nostalgia. No, this is not a pleasure—
nothing is holy in this world. Dare we inhabit
the post-human, a fractal ebb and flow of lymph
and laser. Bless our given bodies without reprisal
or regret: borders we crossed as youth, invisible
at a distance when the fog lifts: no longer home.
Toxic compass rose of exile, carcinogenic blooms.
The land under our soles exudes a bluing perfume,
notes of a failed paradise, of undocumented flight
from zone to sanctuary: exiles fleeing to the allure
of citizenry acquired by sea, by flood, by fire, by war.

DEAR MILLENNIUM, IN TONGUES OF ANGELS

Tongues shimmer in jewels of flame ignited by flint
drilled by angels of the millennium in our minefields
of hiddenness, of syllables flecked by salt and rhyme
feathering midnight's sea caves with dreams of calque,
of alveolar groves budding softly with glottal scent
unfastened on a summer night of rhotic flowers curled
in the darkest throats of the cosmos, of prosody afloat
out of the heavenlies, burning in our thinnest places
where light sighs *yes* and *yes* in the heads of asphodels
with renewed faith, sighing a name, Jesus of Nazareth,
whose love is unchanging, whose charismata, a fluency
of gifting, kindles the xenoglossia of angelic tongues
in this mortal field of furious wishes: yet how can it be
that we hear tongues in our own? Who translates us?
And what do the lilies of the fields say about our brassy
spinning for splendor? What about a bird of the air
winging her way across this wilderness: is this apple
of God's eye, a jelled opening of gentlest humour, also
an edible fruit where light is a ghost uttering *yes*? Flame
after flame, who blesses us? And who mingles this oil
of anointing with praise? If we touch a wounded bell
with mere human hands, surely, woe.

DEAR MILLENNIUM, ON INTERIOR DISCLOSURES

So, millennium, on the ledge of our vanities
this mirroring sea of narcissism, false prophets
languish under aerosol clouds. Faux lagoons
utter the notion, *prosperity*. Our fragility asks
whether scorched war zones are authorized,
if a change in soul-modality from agriculture
to industry
                    drifts from the original genesis
of harmonized, flesh-adorned fruitfulness,
not materialism
or disgrace. Interior disclosures
aren't encrypted sayings, rather, *eat this scroll*,
bright imperatives awakening our bellies.
Attention, dear millennium.   At point-
blank range, God unleashes *miraculum*. Spiritus
Sanctus trains the air to hum notes of myrrh,
no mystery for catastrophe-purified martyrs
                    dipped in boiling oil or eviscerated,
mercy blooming in our globe's flooded hothouse
while a fleet of angelic satellites, orbital wishes,
crash-lands in sub-zero darkness. Dear millennium,
let us sing of crystalline wasps in domed cities
where interior disclosures—whispering *peace*—
speak not of discord, rather, green oxygen
flushing the miniature lungs of doves
as emerald witness.

DEAR MILLENNIUM, ON THE METHUSELAH STAR

The meteor shower, a famous one, arrives tonight.
            To see it, we must drive a hundred miles east
to Joshua Tree, the high desert. The bright Perseids—
            How could we possibly make it
in time, crossing this long, clandestine distance
                to the inland empire?
Past the drought-blighted avocado and lemon groves,
            on cracked, desolate freeways—
A pastor once described our path towards eternity
            as *a long obedience in the same direction.*
Sounds mundane. Even so, I love this austere method of sameness
        while night gently shawls the Mojave with stars—
           ten billion year-old pixie dust
speckling the eastern hemisphere—as our bodies, way stations
        of hydrogen, carbon, and phosphorus atoms
becloud the hairpin-river of the Milky Way
           beyond the light pollution of Los Angeles,
midsummer August. Sea-bright stillness, rose-prickled
             and spectrally red-shifted,
        ancient star fumes
blaze with our unbridled wishes,
        blend with the coiled smoke of gashed comets
barely the age of the oldest star discovered,
        the Methuselah star—
           born fourteen billion years ago.

DEAR MILLENNIUM, ON NINE ORDERS OF ANGELS

Never easily recall the names, dear millennium,
                     of nine angelic orders—
first, ophanims in ocular celestial wheels,
beryl-colored
                     ablaze to the unaided eye,
or else too close to the fire to see a forest aflame,
         blinded in a mentholated sequoia grove.
Second, who are the virtues—
                     celestially distinct
          from angelic hosts, third? Seraphim,
archangels, fourth and fifth. Do you recall?
A dyslexic girl says,
               No-name angel at a taxi corral
rich enough in rags, hatless, without a suitcase,
shone with a clean jaw.
              I offered every penny
out of my purse.
Blessing me, he vanished, coins
         spinning light in light. O heal me.
           Selah.

DEAR MILLENNIUM, ON DAZZLING

Flush of rose-colored ash in the low desert valley
poised on slaked mortar
      where the smog, pillowing out west by freeway,
yields a query. On resurrection day, who will arise
                on this dazzling terrazzo, a walk of fame?
Souls over onyx asphalt? Shall the tawdry, zircon grit of aging glamor
      ascend the fabliaux of violence,
           chrysoprase ocean, indigo zone
of a feckless endgame—on this side, the ring of fire,
of brushfires, short-lived
             sapphire eucalyptus
running out of flame. Burnished loquats. Century agave. Echeveria
        sage rosettes. Salvation
on the side of a chaparral hill in the city of angels and toxic silt,
     forty stories high. Jade-colored car lights in the hunger
of generations moaning in a millennial desert—
      mirages of cucumber, quail, and flesh pots—
insufferable jewelweed
            kisses the glory-cleft, exposed
        xylonite rock of ages at twilight, a darkening glass hour
              of the city's millennial angels.

DEAR MILLENNIUM, ON DEFAMATIONS IN THE METROPOLIS

Dear millennium
    where a vacant red pergola stands
for our annulled decades—

    no bitterness. No bliss. We go to a seaside metropolis
where you sipped xarel wine. Outdoors,
    an impromptu by a Chinese mandolinist and sight-
reading jazz pianist: doppelgängers

        ghosting a minefield of opium angels
who witness your sips of osmanthus wine,
        your kvass of mint, raisins, and berries
    tossed in one sitting
until you lay in gold effervescence. I worried,
    dear
        millennium, you'd die in an epidemic
though I'd virtually eradicated small pox,
    tuberculosis, and rubella
        over the last century.

    Dear millennium of shimmering lights,
I didn't grant you the liberty to roam
        the gallows of roseate carnage
    without releasing you—
        our torrid maze of fire-ladders,
        labyrinths of brass rage in factories,
    operant conditioned responses
to beautiful objects. Or we are socialized
to believe
        anything is beautiful. No. No.

    Dear millennium, now I expect nothing.
After all, what can I glean
    from a million caries in an incorrigible sweet tooth?
        And why persist,

spinning in outer darkness without eyes? Do you see
tattered faces of violets? Do you
cry inwardly while flipping
silver-dollar scallion cakes, agile as glandular
mania in your pockets,
jack-knifed out of squalls, your narcissism? Are you
ever forced into polarities? Are you a whim
of chance, or a bruised planet of intelligent design,
stuttering
in a phantasmagoria of liquidated assets
amassed by billionaires?

Say a volatile currency is worth saving in this famine—
a yuan's cherry-coal banknote, of the day before yesterday's
smoke-plumed petals of Shanghai,
tomorrow's algorithms
of indeterminacy?
Only confess: this lovely megacity is savage—

DEAR MILLENNIUM, OUR HUNGRY ROSES

Dear millennium, our hungry roses
dissolve ounces of bone-meal at your feet, harnessing
light into polysaccharides—
oblivious to water-use restriction in drought, as if tasting
raw joy for the sake of rivers would save us—
not forty subclavian nights in a global flood,
not stones-as-bread forsaken in a Judaean desert
in the company of angels, only scorched ravines plunging
to pseudo-fossilized ire
without traces of ferns or dendrites.
Besotted in the torrid rose garden, engorged with honeysap,
aphids do not care whether a famine rages in our land.
Should I confess, dear millennium? Chrysopoeia is nothing to do
with levitating beautiful objects, unless we count
transmuting the figurative into gold.
I thirst. You hunger. There is no special alchemy of grace—
everything is clearly spelled.
For he shall give his angels charge over thee, to keep you
in all your ways. They shall bear you up in their hands,
lest you dash your foot against a stone.

DEAR MILLENNIUM, ON THE DEBT OF LOVE AMONG STRANGERS

Dear millennium, my pragmatic love—
If I wax quixotic in fanciful figures of speech,
you wish to discuss our finances.

In our provinces of raw silk clouds,
is it a myth that silk once was used as currency?
A sack of flour costs a day's wages

while surplus monies trigger inflation—
zillions exchanged for typing paper, nephrite,
fish sauce, rock salt, or tea bags

in a time of shortage. Gasoline
is no longer a fragrance in the national treasuries,
nor the debt of love a perfume—

more we offer, the more we carry.
No dollars reinvested in good faith
as a form of heavenly currency.

Once I told you, love is a partial
anagram of solvency. Dear millennium, please—
I owe you nothing.

I do not love you as a stranger.
I do not shun you as a post-war mine field
or an atom bomb. I love you

as any comrade-in-arms in a season
of rationing, in our taxed gardens of austerity
sparing only a tithe of light.

DEAR MILLENNIUM, ON WEATHER ALERTS AS DOXOLOGY

Praise God for the cool sea fog wafting
       in swatches over my face,
presaging a rain squall, the slashing bands
       of cloudy water moving over a sea.
I boiled a pot of rice in severe weather,
       forgot to close my window,
so the rain pooled on the floor.
       My own rain factory, I laughed—
to manufacture weather like a shop,
       let it inhabit my domestic spaces—
a friendly cloud who follows children.
       The clouds warn us of the second coming,
clouds beckon us to prayer. Come in,
       come in. Enter into the holiest
of holies, into the glory cloud.
       Yesterday, creeks and canyons flooded—
cross winds pushed water over the peninsula,
       dangerous surf at high tide. If you recall
the dry months last year, when honeysuckle
       curled back in the heat, and a non-fruiting
olive tree touched the sand with its thirst,
       this rainfall is a blessing—
even worms peep from their earth-holes
       to inspect the armored locusts,
and the heavenly host rolls in its bed,
       the softest velvet field of clover,
starry buds tuned to the sky's swollen moods
       before a battery of storm alerts,
small prophets of eschatological climate change.

       Let us praise God for what we know
only in this realm, the uncertainty of weather,
       neither conquered nor contained.

DEAR MILLENNIUM, ON RADIO WAVES

A shelf of clouds moves low and gold above us—
        a loved one's voice echoes far away, yet not too far,
near enough to scent the winter air with rain
        from within, a soul in the rootage of an oak

with lights strung, and a shower of azaleas
        more bloom than leaf by blue-edged camellias
so bright they blush if you say their names,
        a row of wild roses running strong as cables

edging the bay where sage-colored tree hair
        tangles on the mottled arms of pond pines—
the hush of those trees mingled with sweet gum
        calms us the same way a fog drops

over an eight-mile bayway until the sky vanishes
        on the other side. There are bridges in the world
longer than ours, and piers wrecked countless times
        by the force of hurricane winds, rebuilt by hand—

this is the end of times as our gospel radio
        airs the reports of weather and good news
over waters so quiet, no one would presage storms—
        this is the way we push out to the gulf stream

where God waits on the other side, we surmise,
        in a body of jubilee without sorrow, a man
whose blade chopped wood, whose bare soles
        blessed the soil with sweet olives flowering

in gardens reeling with perfume, who bled
        for our little deaths, for the sake of love
on this side of this life, who opened glory for us
        rolling past this present tide.

DEAR MILLENNIUM, FIGS SAY HUNGER ALONE IS NOT THE BODY

                Do not
begrudge a season of flying ants,
when the figs
flower.
– Please forgive us.
A body glows with milk and sage-honey—
             ravenous. Hunger
       raps on our pergola, out in the cold.
       Olive oil in a communion glass
gleams as though holiness
       poured once.
             No one ever partook.

Fig thieves scour a winter grove,
redwood-boned,
while gull-colored magnolias
bleed from the pips. Bear no witness.
          Honeybees do not solve
puzzles on vanishing,
      beetle-pollinated opulence
by the fireweed,
    as a bee colony declines little by little
this century.
       Why is beauty
         warring to wreck
       a scurf of moss, crabgrass
or wild mallow in a gutter?
Thieves in the garden—
       among fig trees with elephantine leaves—
         recalling milky light
under violet-black fig skin, stolen
– *those figs never were sweet.*

In girlhood, our coastal mesa
       flooded,

garden walls visible
        only to flaming angels of paradise.
Afterward, the fruit orchard was bitter—a thief
confesses—
Once I picked a fig
        skinned to the core—a bruise.
What occurs when you hold a bruise
             to the light?
Does flesh oxidize?
Does it shrivel and darken,
        pressed in cakes
sown every winter
          to flower without ire
in the afterlife? How does it heal?

        – The figs say, hunger alone
is not the body.

DEAR MILLENNIUM, ON THE ANGEL
OF IMMIGRATION

In the skin of your rain-mottled angel of immigration
who looks forward
               with a diamond clasp
      of upward mobility on her watery clavicle,

                     inner rain called *mizzle* is shining—

a chrome-polishing rag
                        on a bicycle while the fig tree
loses its foliage due to a blight called *rust*. Dear millennium,
                  destined to be a girl,
artist or engineer,
you've never fallen in love. (Do you even believe?) Centuries,

                  this peace offering—

a non-fruiting olive
                  transplanted
                        after your lavender died of root-rot
      on a winter afternoon in the north.

      (Day after a sea storm, holy
and granular—
               bayside hailing clean off the rim, napthlalene
                        stored in mothless air,
agelessness, hybrid tea-roses, and rocket fuel.)

            Ear-shaped, honey-combed morels
flourish by the rosemary, edible yet uneaten—
                  dearly so, as evidence

of a battered dictionary you once loved. (Light-drenched sea,
      its charismatic splendor, is a room
                           of meticulous self-reform,
                  noxious blue-eyed madness
of the dead.) For this reason, your ancestors
                  wished to sail on a ship around a landform
      to its southernmost point. (Dear millennium, what we loved

is written tenderly in the dregs of the earth.)
Dear millennium, see how immigrants
              yearn for departure and extravagance,
freedom with a notion of rootedness.
          In this generational reimagining, dear millennium—
we are cured of nothing
                  yet everything at once.

DEAR MILLENNIUM, A JADE RABBIT ON THE FAR SIDE OF THE MOON

We sent a rover called Jade Rabbit to the far side of our moon,
the other side of hiddenness as it faces away from this world,
where cotton seeds sprouted at first, but don't expect the moon
to change into fresh cotton fields soon, thanks to airlessness—
minus subzero in microgravity, absolutely freezing up there.
The spacecraft which carried the rover was named for a lady
who drank the elixir of immortality and floated to the moon.
She was the same lady who married the archer who shot nine
of the ten suns scorching the earth. As a little girl, I wondered
if the lady was bored out of her wits from sitting on the moon,
a blanched, cold place without almond cakes or green cheese.
The moon is not made of jade, either. Of course, you can't eat
jade, but it is soothing to hold. Meanwhile, the moon's far side
lies in utter darkness due to tidal locking, not what it sounds—
actually the moon's orbit and its rotation are not about oceans
the way we feel the ebb and flow of their familiar nocturnes.
The darkness is more about not knowing what else is there.
It is also not quite the opposite of what we do see, however.
Don't expect that the moon will turn into cotton fields soon.
It is not made of mutton fat. Neither cassia trees nor rabbits
dwell there. On the far side, we find what we already know—
that seeds cannot survive in such weather, and sadly, we get
no closer to knowing God in doing so, not even in reaching
out to graze the edges of the farthest stars, dear millennium,
when God is shooting valentines of love into jaded hearts
where strings hold our atoms of flesh together, for now.

DEAR MILLENNIUM, LOVE

Dear millennium, love—a postscript,
        would you please translate
dying languages   into living
tongues?
        Dear universe of destroying angels,

please minimize the risks
            of our bioethical quandaries shot
thru by doubt,
        of joy shining on liquid crystal,

transfiguration
    of penny operas
                into brass-toned pyrite
seeking paranoia-free sums of grace

                in metaphysical drops of gold

                        pressed
olive oil anointing our gall-soaked martyrologies,

flame-treasures of Christ. Yes, a beleaguered
widow   offered all she had

in a prophetic exchange, as even now our poverty
                is the currency of heaven—

Were not our hearts burning within us
        when he spoke to us on the road?

Dear angels of destruction in a post-religious age,
    dare we say, this conservatory of hunger
        feeds a debris-field of ash? Flashes of torn
                    lilacs? Dear red azaleas,

bombed-out subways, dashed portals of aroma
        in blown-out train stations

           dancing on faceless shards of cola
glass

    who are no longer—*Everything is falling.*

Dear ugliest taste of plumed diesel
    shot back to shorn towers,   our
civilization

     of *not there*   rain. River. Bay.
       Dear late daylilies lasting bizzarely,

millennial angels loiter on a fire escape
    in fractured abecedarian light, our lettered
       A B C D avenues in disarray. *Selah.*

ON MERIDIANS OF LOVE AND DISTANCE 4

ON MERIDIANS OF LOVE AND DISTANCE

What's on the other side of the ocean we wonder
as we stroll on the far edge of the sea cliffs at dusk
above the tidal erosion of caves, of watery coves
gouged like eye sockets of centuries, a vanishing
witness to their own passing? I guess San Clemente
or Catalina, the Islas Coronados of gulls, the noun
azimuth on a reference plane of this giant sphere
where jeweled lights of night-fishing boats float
on gibbous waters of a mirrored summer moon,
and you reply, *I meant a landmass,* if we're south
of Shanghai or Miyazaki on the same latitude,
a planet circumscribing Istanbul, Baghdad,
Damascus, Tripoli, Atlanta, Phoenix, Dallas,
at last plunging through the San Diego desert
where dividing meridians and invisible parallels
delineate our planet by angle or degree, intimate
curves of the earth, the longing distances of time
passing through us like arrows or nautical stars
guiding our hearts with mortal roses of weather,
our flesh windroses arrayed in cardinal directions—
love, prayer, light, then love again, singing
north, south, east, and west.

ON JUNE BLOSSOMING IN JUNE

This summer, we drank cardamom iced tea sweetened with agave—
savoring an idea of sweetness lingering, not as if we actually ate honey
from the lovely overflow of liquid summer heat and soft beeswax
tongued with a wedge of spanakopita and a platter of shaved lamb
    strewn on pita bread with yogurt cucumber dip—
glistening slices of salmon topped by edamame, wakame seaweed,
crushed macadamia nuts mingled with black sesame on beds of rice,
and steaming cups of chai with black tea and milk, loose-leaf sencha,
and chunks of sea bass with a tossed mesclun of tender greens
    garnished by crisp curls of chicharrones
and chopped beet salad with tart beets—the mellow gold ones
soaked in wine vinegar, dressed with tendrils of microgreens—
corollas of night-blooming honeysuckle and star jasmine flaming
with small cups of heady fumes wafting on trellises across the lot
    with a walk-in hair salon and laundromat—
then avocados with eggs-over-easy in hollandaise sauce over muffins
alongside triangles of toast dipped in yolks beaten with cinnamon,
    and flavorful black coffee with a drop of fresh cream,
quiche with crimini mushrooms, feta, swiss cheese, not leeks or truffles,
shot through with julienned sundried tomatoes the color of stop signs,
and mocha spiced with chili, black pepper, chocolate, cardamom again
by a plate of smoked salmon and capers, ricotta, buttery arugula,
and baby spinach drizzled with olive oil on thin sourdough toast
    in glowing strokes of late June light
fringed by the noise of peninsula traffic on the harbor
    laced by grease and silt from the machinery of life—
the sea isn't far away though only gulls could spy it from here—
so why don't we walk all the way to the inlet of the marina, a landing
where children play in the fading light blanched on grassy edges
    as if already a memory of summer within summer—
and you say, with the air of a prophet who ate locusts and honey,
join me in the place where lives are bound together
    by a cord of three strands.

SONG OF THE OYAMEL

On the other side of this door
You are an oyamel native to the mountains of Michoacan

Rising in a cloud-forest of sister evergreens
Shedding pollen-cones, shedding winged seeds

Our lost wings
        singly and in pairs.

This is why the monarchs vanish
Raising sienna-hued colonies longer than my arms

Hibernating in Mexico where it's hotter in January
        than my front yard, where the red bougainvillea raves

And magnolias   with a mauve rush on paper

And open as though thinking about last year's novels

Read over the shoulders of garden-strollers

Obey the apostle's exhortation
And do everything in love.

ON LUCID DREAMING

To experience lucid dreaming, a body must lie still, arms at sides
for at least twenty minutes, breathing evenly, dismissing the impulse
to swallow. After only five minutes, my flesh slid into another state
as my thoughts slowed, beta waves to alpha waves, but I broke a rule—
I opened my eyes. The ceiling fan on, the lamp with the energy-saving
bulb free of mercury vapor, the windchime with a cedar pendulum
I brought indoors, and a family of angels with words in granite,
peace, love, and *tranquility.* Not one even started dreaming,
and neither did I, never mind lucidly. I arose to look up the parts
of a windchime and realized *pendulum* is not one. O-ring, clapper,
and dreamcatcher, also known as a feather.

ON LECTIO DIVINA, COUNTER-CLOCKWISE

Both hands of a clock rotate counter-clockwise
as I read backwards—*you, give, leave, I, peace.*
You gave us peace. You left us peace. You left
us for a little while until you returned, glorified
in an era without aerial shots, prior to montage.
A figurative clock I mentioned is anachronistic.
You said, *Peace I leave you. My peace I give you.*
Where is a criminal's memory of your last hour,
quaking midnight of an olive tree in the nerves,
flesh-pit of soil engendered by God, yet son of man
not without yearning? Yes, I visited a nook where
I was birthed, a rough labor. Read about you
without knowing your love. *Peace I leave you.*
You left us your serenity

                         not as the world gives.
Nothing I do can deliver me from my own folly.
When this basin of hunger pours its shame,
even my blunt senses touch a healing salve—

         without fragrance or blight,
         your pseudo-absence

                 is holy presence—
blotted rosettas on a chilled ledge
under linen, seventy-five pounds of aloe, myrrh,
your lungs ninety-percent sea, nine percent
Nazareth well-water. Who are we

            to say what is pure,
this marvelous opening
onto light.

ON BLESSING LENTILS

I can do without

fresh rosemary,
pureed squash,
even red onion

in place of vidalia.
I can do without dill
or sage

if only cumin seeds
remain. I can do
without tomatoes

and ham-hocks.
However, I cannot
do without

the last broth
saved from a roast,
or lentils—

the basis
of the stew. Thank you
for flavoring

this provision
with salt.
Amen.

ODE TO THE LONGEST PIER ON THE LEFT COAST

In the gutted fish-light of early morning, of anglers
casting their lines out to a cold, crushed sea of kelp
waving under a shuttered bistro floating a phrase,
walking on water, on its marquee, I count streets

sloping down to the bluffs, eight named for cities
and forests: santa monica, saratoga, cape may,
long branch avenue, muir and lotus, sunset cliffs,
then a boulevard, east to west. Three nights ago,

you said, a car spun off into the darkness of the pier—
fixed last year with city funds—hit two pedestrians
before spinning into the streets again. Intoxication.
Why else would a person drive right onto the wharf?

Who would execute such a brutal plan, then smile
with a blissful look on his face, as bystanders said?
Why does our world birth equal parts recklessness
and harm? Couldn't God hold us in a starry hand,

soothe us with salves of mystical glue, heal us
instantaneously, our lives ineluctably scarred
by misadventures? You ask frankly whether
I should continue spending time with you

while you're taking me to dangerous places—
two bystanders in a ruthless, dangerous world
rife with toxic, unholy places riddled by risk.
We wonder if some places are safer than others,

or is this a fear of losing oneself utterly in a soul
of another, where one can't find a way back
from the stairless fathoms without a loyal torch
to light the way? In other words, if we abandon

ourselves to ourselves without stepping out
on the endless waves of a beatific design

beyond charted waters, we must especially
pray we must know it.

MEDITATION ON SOTERIOLOGY

I confess the obvious, my inadequacy to translate
famine to bread to feed all the hungry children on earth.
Wish I could invent a happiness machine or dollar tree

blossoming with non-taxable revenue for small businesses.
Wish for a thousand bitcoins, wild doves of aqueous tongues,
non-walled paradises of flora and flame, psalms of untilled
ardor, testimonies on fevered ink-stone. Inner voice says,
Aren't you asking whether there is a soul

        or whether souls may be saved?

Wish I could do more than arrange inklings into lines,
whisper God's love into our millennial vanity as labor.
Wish I cobbled heels of solace at funerals for mothers.
In a vision, Jesus is younger than I am now, bleeding
on iron pikes driven to bone. See a letter in the shape
of a T square, pin on pin. Wonderful how he fulfills
his divine assignment, what he is called to do. Night
drops like a black lily—

        the labor is finished.

A LIGHTHOUSE ON THIS SIDE OF LIFE

On our drive to the southern tip of a peninsula
       overlooking islands named Shelter and Harbor
by Coronado translated in Spanish as crowned
       of the sea, under a lone cloud floating over a lookout
on the sea cliff, by a path winding
       to a lighthouse fringed by lemongrass, rosemary,
chard, oregano, kale, spinach, and thyme in a fenced garden,
       of jeweled lenses glowing like a round-shouldered girl
with a graceful youth spied through a looking glass
       in a world where a spiral stair turns like an ear
pressed to heaven humming shaft after shaft of light
       above a rain catchment basin
the length of a lighthouse's shadow pointing to the water
       where we'd watch the bay merging with the sea—
you asked, *where are we going, where have we been,*
       seeing flowers and signs of life along the path?
Nettle and black sage and sugar bush and fiddleneck,
       feverfew and elderberry and mule fat—
your childhood memories of playing bughouse
       while drinking jars of sweet tea into late nights,
stars shining in a field like marbles
       smooth as headstones
held to the inner bones of our bodies
         younger than rare pines billowing
       in the lightness of skirts or guardian angels—
         if we gaze at faraway stars long enough,
we'll see circles and roses, then crosses and stars
       with those years of life engraved row on row,
        a gentle slope facing the sea
where my ancestors on the other shore once believed
       it was auspicious *fengshui* to be buried in a place
        where wind, mountains, and water meet
face to face with a foretaste of eternity
          on this side of life.

ON THE TURNING OF THE YEAR

To witness five seventeen-year cicada
cycles in a lifetime—To hear an entomologist refer to cycles
        as *blooms*—

To say a metallic clicking noise repels the crows in our apple
orchard—To say cicada *blooms* explain the crashing
        bird populations—

To list reasons why I wish to murmur injunctions of praise
in the ellipses of fireflies—To wonder if a funicular
           monikered *angel flight,*

rusted out-of-commission on a city hill,
           a mourning dove over beds of grass-licked cloud,
hovers—

To ponder the alpha and omega of eating

        salmon roe—To sing the floating syllables of winter suns—
trilling rose-fire of melisma—

To arrange star-gazer lilies on a console so a day
        brightens—To seek an equivalent for *nonexistence*
           not *absence*—

        To pray until we vanish together, in sum—
        To say without song, *hosanna*—at the turning of the year

ON RADIOGENIC MINERALS IN OUR HEARTS

In a grain of sand, the half-lives of our years vanish ahead,
radiogenic minerals of quartz and feldspar, iodine's isotopes
decaying in the seas of radiance shimmering, our bodies.
A day of the year passes over us like an unspoken ghost
in this incandescent room, the aerosol skies of this hour,

the tales of our fates and future loves carved in our hands—
remember azaleas stripped to leaf by a single rainstorm,
jacaranda carpets mixing pleasure with phosphorescence,
beetle-pollinated magnolias sighing by the slough, echoing
rooftop farolitos illuminating the months of solstice dark—

and you ask, *why did the southern dogwood bloom so early
in late winter,* unfolding a shaggy float of crucifix petals
surreal as a jeweled seahorse on a pedestal in a boutique
or a flowering mimosa anchored on a bright, encircling shore
shedding reams of cotton-tuft flowers, offering soft plumes

of solace for those who lost keys at the turquoise cantina
by a little dog beach where I cast off my summer flats
to walk on the noonday sand as if rising over the hot coals
of a wayfaring heart, this garnet trench of stirred embers
burning with questions. How do the hours pass to quicken

the years spent together, regardless of our dogged path
of beautiful irony? You say, *one day, this will pass,
yet the foundation will remain, and so will we.* I show
how the fingertips of my hands touch only the first joint
on each of yours.

ON REVERSE PAROUSIA, THE SEQUEL

I guess we only go up once,
no coming back.

Not in the sense of bird flight,
ripped chiffon or cotton frocks.
Rolled in a tsunami,

wave of the Holy Spirit
takes no life. In this case,
we abandon this realm.

No one knows where we vanished,
spilling cups of green tea
or how we, too, purblind

about yesterday
kept our shale-formed lamps
oiled with hope.

I know a stranger
will see marks on this page,
ask, what if lost loved ones

come in a reverse arrival
to populate the world,
magnolias sown to bloom.

Do we sip tea at the return?
Valerian for insomnia
at night, not knowing when?

We box our books if a quake
liquefies our zone, or a tsunami
unspools from grace.

As for the second coming—

ON THE YOUNGEST FILAMENT IN THE UNIVERSE

And how young is this universe? Centuries ago,
paper currency in circulation for the first time—

yet this is not old. Planets, hoary and garish,
                    ignited like ships overseas—

and are mere infants. Even in our epoch,
of surveillance, a comet
                        explodes unseen. An asteroid

the size of a washing machine, captured
by the earth's orbit, is dubbed—
            little sister to the moon or mini-moon.

The youngest filament in the universe is a forest
of hydrogen, light years across,

fattened by molecular rivers of gas, the inklings
of super structures held by gravity.

Is the human heart any less healed or scarred
than it was eons ago?

Our aspirations are much newer than atoms
or galaxy filaments
                    tracing an arc to the future—

closer than yesterday, this cardiac nanosecond
brushed ash and star-grit from our lives

most dazzling after sunset—
                        youngest right now.

MEDITATION ON THE END OF ALL THINGS

Our noon is the last one in April, a Saturday.

What we call star-jasmines

night-blooming

bless a south wind on its way to the ocean, so I test the air.

One by one, engines of scent hum on the mesa.

Annually, this season, nocturnal jasmines wake. And honeysuckle.

Months of green: green.

August prunes blooming back until only September sings

on the edges. November, still green.

Through March, no other than green.

May: thousands open

floss-strung, starry tangles of aroma. Laced on fumes, I pick none

honoring what we do not know   or dare not
surmise:

the end of all things is near.

ON LIGHTENING

Not sure whether this fire-rimmed moon, bowled rose of hunger
is due to solar radiation or aging.

This day, the nineteenth of July, a wild hare leaps into a fire
a thousand times. I am not yet forty years old.

My hair grows to shoulder length and longer
than my shoulder blades under a cassia on the moon

of alabaster halls lined with mochi cakes, red quinoa,
radish seeds popping

their claret skins. From this day on, I no longer wish to go
without sole almondine. In a many-roomed mansion

with a one-eyed monocle, I will look back on this day
as one where I decided to live
lightly
                this summer on.

My hair is lighter.
It lightens in the darkness of firs.

DEAR MILLENNIUM, OF EDIBLE BLOSSOMS AND THE UNBORN

The unborn who never make it into this world are edible
blossoms in the orphic throat of God, garlanded by floral
seraphs. Yes, the sky-blue borage, the cilantro and fennel
and calendula, the crystallized viola and skirted zucchini,
the alyssum and the fava bean flowers, even the dahlia—
the micro-fuchsia, and the dianthus, the garlic and chive,
the ox-eyed sun-daisy, the shiso blossoms for mint julep,
chiffonade garnish of sage and sorrel of ribboned jade,
the umbels of onion blooms, the six-petaled bell pepper
florets of nightshade, the hibiscus without hips, the ice
plant flourishing on sea cliffs where I touched sweet pea
entwined within the chaparral understory where a sand
lizard, a brother who never came to be, who lost his tail
before he was born, greets me every afternoon while sun
bathing, his missing appendage reblooming with aplomb,
as if admonishing our millennium with apostolic fervor—
in lumine tuo videbimus lumen, in your light we see light.

POSTSCRIPT TO DEAR MILLENNIUM, LOVE

Before I fell asleep last night, a double-star conjunction
shone so blindly, I fished it out of the west

with a rag of spider silk lost by the woolly bold jumper.
Please fix my bandwidth
                so I do more sensible things.

Your skyscrapers, after falling, are going up, jagged
        scapes, in a nanosecond,

scaffolded and realigned as smoke. Millennium
of burned, hairless marigolds,
        of moonquakes, grenades

and dazzling insects not lasting the night: we grant ourselves
permission for intimacy, for freedom to choose

whom we love while on earth
              even if we do not love whom we ought—

ENDNOTES

"On Floriography" was arranged for voice and piano by composer Tony Payne and performed by Sarah Holman (mezzo-soprano) and Karin Edwards (piano) at Wheaton College. This poem first appeared in the Poem-a-Day feature sponsored by the Academy of American Poets.

"Prayer in the Year of No Rain" was inspired by "California Drought." State of California. 6 June 2014. Web. http://www.ca.gov/drought/

*

"The Last Bookstore in the World" refers to California's largest used book and records store, "The Last Bookstore," located on Spring Street in Los Angeles.

*

"Irenology:" *As deep calls to deep* is quoted from Psalm 42:7, *New International Version.*

*

"Petty Skills Like the Carving of Insects:" The title phrase is mentioned by Yan Hsiung, qtd. on p. 118 in James Liu's *Chinese Theories of Literature.* Chicago: University of Chicago Press, 1975.

The following lines are excerpted from *Discipline and Punish: The Birth of the Prison* by Michel Foucault. Alan Sheridan, trans. New York: Vintage, 1995.

. . . an uninterrupted work of writing . . . (197)

. . . linking the center and periphery . . . (197)

. . . in which the slightest movements are supervised (197)

The following lines are quoted from poems carved into the wood barracks on Angel Island, translated and collected by Him Mark Lai, Genny Lim, and Judy Yung. *Island: Poetry and History of Chinese Immigrants on Angel Island, 1910-1940.* Washington: University of Washington Press, 1991.

. . . the ocean has changed into a mulberry grove . . . . (Mr. Ruan, p. 60)

...I have no words to murmur against the east wind .... (Mr. Ruan, p. 60)

... My body is detained in this building .... (Mr. Ruan, p. 60)

... It was not easy finding space on the wall .... (Mr. Ng, age 15 in 1931, p. 136)

... because the wood there was softer .... (Mr. Ng, age 15 in 1931, p. 136)

... wherever the hand could reach .... (Mr. Ng, age 15 in 1931, p. 136)

... Even if it is built of jade, it has turned into a cage. (Anonymous, p. 134)

*

"Song of the Oyamel:" Oyamel, in Nahuatl, means "sacred fir." *And do everything in love* is quoted from 1 Corinthians 16:14, *New Living Translation*. Tyler Heckman arranged this poem for voice and piano while studying at Missouri State University. This poem first appeared in *Poetry*.

*

"On the Youngest Filament in the Universe" was inspired by "Faint Filaments of Universe-Spanning 'Cosmic Web' Finally Found." Read more at https://www.space.com/universe-cosmic-web-filaments-found.html

*

"On the Turning of the Year" was featured on the Slow Down Show hosted by Tracy K. Smith. This poem first appeared in *Spoon River Poetry Review*.

A recipient of an NEA grant, Karen An-hwei Lee is the author of five poetry collections, including *Phyla of Joy* (Tupelo Press) and *In Medias Res* (Sarabande Books).

RECENT AND SELECTED TITLES
FROM TUPELO PRESS

Small Altars by Justin Gardiner

Country Songs for Alice by Emma Binder

Asterism by Ae Hee Lee

then telling be the antidote by Xiao Yue Shan

Therapon by Bruce Bond & Dan Beachy-Quick

membery by Preeti Kaur Rajpal

How To Live by Kelle Groom

Sleep Tight Satellite by Carol Guess

THINE by Kate Partridge

The Future Will Call You Something Else by Natasha Sajé

Night Logic by Matthew Gellman

The Unreal City by Mike Lala

Wind—Mountain—Oak: Poems of Sappho Dan Beachy-Quick, Trans.

Tender Machines by J. Mae Barizo

Best of Tupelo Quarterly Kristina Marie Darling, Ed.

We Are Changed to Deer at the Broken Place by Kelly Weber

Why Misread a Cloud by Emily Carlson

The Strings Are Lightning and Hold You In by Chee Brossy

Ore Choir: The Lava on Iceland by Katy Didden and Kevin Tsang

The Air in the Air Behind It by Brandon Rushton

The Future Perfect: A Fugue by Eric Pankey

American Massif by Nicholas Regiacorte

City Scattered by Tyler Mills

Today in the Taxi by Sean Singer

April at the Ruins by Lawrence Raab

The Many Deaths of Inocencio Rodriguez by Iliana Rocha

The Lantern Room by Chloe Honum

Love Letter to Who Owns the Heavens by Corey Van Landingham

Glass Bikini by Kristin Bock